vay
p the day,
piple your spoo,
ne ya do.

THE HUNTING OF THE SNARK

LEWIS CARROLL

The Hunting of the Snark

An Agony in Eight fits

(Illustrated by Mervyn Peake)

CHATTO & WINDUS

LONDON

This edition published in 1993 by
Chatto & Windus Ltd
20 Vauxhall Bridge Road
London SW1V 2SA

First published by Chatto & Windus Ltd in 1941

A CIP catalogue record for this book is available from the
British Library.

ISBN 0 7011 6052 7

Printed in Great Britain by
Butler & Tanner Ltd, Frome and London

CONTENTS

PREFACE

IF——AND the thing is wildly possible——the charge of writing nonsense were ever brought against the author of this brief but Instructive poem, it would be based, I feel convinced, on the line (in p. 11)

"Then the bowsprit got mixed with the rudder sometimes."

In view of this painful possibility, I will not (as I might) appeal indignantly to my other writings as a proof that I am incapable of such a deed: I will not (as I might) point to the strong moral purpose of this poem itself, to the arithmetical principles so cautiously inculcated in it, or to its noble teachings in Natural History——I will take the more prosaic course of simply explaining how it happened.

The Bellman, who was almost morbidly sensitive about appearances, used to have the bowsprit unshipped once or twice a week to be revarnished, and it more than once happened, when the time came for replacing it, that no one on board could remember which end of the ship it belonged to. They knew it was not of the slightest use to appeal to the Bellman about it——he would only refer to his Naval Code, and read out in pathetic tones Admiralty Instructions which none of them had ever been able to understand——so it generally ended in its being fastened on, anyhow, across the rudder. The helmsman[1] used to stand by with tears in his eyes: *he* knew it was all wrong, but alas! Rule 42 of the Code, "*No one shall speak to the Man at the Helm,*" had been completed by the Bellman himself with the words "*and the Man at the Helm shall speak to no one.*" So remonstrance was impossible, and no steering could be done till the next varnishing day. During these bewildering intervals the ship usually sailed backwards.

As this poem is to some extent connected with the lay of the Jabberwock, let me take this opportunity of answering a question that has often been asked me, how to pronounce "slithy toves." The "i" in "slithy" is long, as in "writhe"; and "toves" is pronounced so as to rhyme with "groves." Again, the first "o" in "borogoves" is pronounced like the "o" in "borrow." I have heard people try to give it the sound of the "o" in "worry." Such is Human Perversity.

This also seems a fitting occasion to notice the other hard words in that poem. Humpty-Dumpty's theory, of two

---

[1] This office was usually undertaken by the Boots, who found in it a refuge from the Baker's constant complaints about the insufficient blacking of his three pair of boots.

meanings packed into one word like a portmanteau, seems to me the right explanation for all.

For instance, take the two words "fuming" and "furious." Make up your mind that you will say both words, but leave it unsettled which you will say first. Now open your mouth and speak. If your thoughts incline ever so little towards "fuming," you will say "fuming-furious"; if they turn, by even a hair's breadth, towards "furious," you will say "furious-fuming"; but if you have that rarest of gifts, a perfectly balanced mind, you will say "frumious."

Supposing that, when Pistol uttered the well known words—

"Under which king, Bezonian? Speak or die!"

Justice Shallow had felt certain that it was either William or Richard, but had not been able to settle which, so that he could not possibly say either name before the other, can it be doubted that, rather than die, he would have gasped out "Rilchiam!"

FIT THE FIRST
The Landing

"Just the place for a Snark!" the Bellman cried,
   As he landed his crew with care;
Supporting each man on the top of the tide
   By a finger entwined in his hair.

"Just the place for a Snark!   I have said it twice:
   That alone should encourage the crew.
Just the place for a Snark!   I have said it thrice:
   What I tell you three times is true."

The crew was complete: it included a Boots—
   A maker of Bonnets and Hoods—
A Barrister, brought to arrange their disputes—
   And a Broker, to value their goods.

A Billiard-marker, whose skill was immense,
    Might perhaps have won more than his share—
But a Banker, engaged at enormous expense,
    Had the whole of their cash in his care.

There was also a Beaver, that paced on the deck,
    Or would sit making lace in the bow:
And had often (the Bellman said) saved them
        from wreck,
    Though none of the sailors knew how.

There was one who was famed for the number
        of things
    He forgot when he entered the ship:
His umbrella, his watch, all his jewels and rings,
    And the clothes he had bought for the trip.

He had forty-two boxes, all carefully packed,
    With his name painted clearly on each:
But, since he omitted to mention the fact,
    They were all left behind on the beach.

The loss of his clothes hardly mattered, because
   He had seven coats on when he came,
With three pair of boots——but the worst of
     it was,
   He had wholly forgotten his name.

He would answer to "Hi!" or to any loud cry,
   Such as "Fry me!" or "Fritter my wig!"
To "What-you-may-call-um!" or "What-was-his-
     name!"
   But especially "Thing-um-a-jig!"

While, for those who preferred a more forcible
     word,
   He had different names from these:
His intimate friends called him "Candle-ends,"
   And his enemies "Toasted-cheese."

"His form is ungainly——his intellect small——"
   (So the Bellman would often remark)
"But his courage is perfect!   And that, after all,
   Is the thing that one needs with a Snark."

He would joke with hyænas, returning their stare
   With an impudent wag of the head:
And he once went a walk, paw-in-paw, with a bear,
   "Just to keep up its spirits," he said.

He came as a Baker: but owned when too late—
   And it drove the poor Bellman half-mad—
He could only bake Bridecake——for which, I may
    state,
   No materials were to be had.

The last of the crew needs especial remark,
   Though he looked an incredible dunce:
He had just one idea——but, that one being "Snark,"
   The good Bellman engaged him at once.

He came as a Butcher: but gravely declared,
   When the ship had been sailing a week,
He could only kill Beavers.   The Bellman looked
    scared,
   And was almost too frightened to speak:

But at length he explained, in a tremulous tone,
    There was only one Beaver on board;
And that was a tame one he had of his own,
    Whose death would be deeply deplored.

The Beaver, who happened to hear the remark,
    Protested, with tears in its eyes,
That not even the rapture of hunting the Snark
    Could atone for that dismal surprise!

It strongly advised that the Butcher should be
    Conveyed in a separate ship:
But the Bellman declared that would never agree
    With the plans he had made for the trip:

Navigation was always a difficult art,
    Though with only one ship and one bell:
And he feared he must really decline, for his part,
    Undertaking another as well.

The Beaver's best course was, no doubt, to procure
    A second-hand dagger-proof coat——

So the Baker advised it——and next, to insure
  Its life in some Office of note:

This the Baker suggested, and offered for hire
    (On moderate terms), or for sale,
Two excellent Policies, one Against Fire,
    And one Against Damage From Hail.

Yet still, ever after that sorrowful day,
    Whenever the Butcher was by,
The Beaver kept looking the opposite way,
    And appeared unaccountably shy.

FIT THE SECOND
The Bellman's Speech

The Bellman himself they all praised to the skies—
    Such a carriage, such ease and such grace!
Such solemnity, too!   One could see he was wise,
    The moment one looked in his face!

He had bought a large map representing the sea,
    Without the least vestige of land:
And the crew were much pleased when they found it
      to be
    A map they could all understand.

"What's the good of Mercator's North Poles and
      Equators,
    Tropics, Zones, and Meridian Lines?"

So the Bellman would cry: and the crew would reply
    "They are merely conventional signs!

"Other maps are such shapes, with their islands
        and capes!
    But we've got our brave Captain to thank"
(So the crew would protest) "that he's bought us
        the best——
    A perfect and absolute blank!"

This was charming, no doubt: but they shortly
        found out
    That the Captain they trusted so well
Had only one notion for crossing the ocean,
    And that was to tingle his bell.

He was thoughtful and grave——but the orders he
        gave
    Were enough to bewilder a crew.
When he cried "Steer to starboard, but keep her
        head larboard!"
    What on earth was the helmsman to do?

Then the bowsprit got mixed with the rudder
    sometimes:
    A thing, as the Bellman remarked,
That frequently happens in tropical climes,
    When a vessel is, so to speak, "snarked."

But the principal failing occurred in the sailing,
    And the Bellman, perplexed and distressed,
Said he *had* hoped, at least, when the wind blew due
    East
    That the ship would *not* travel due West!

But the danger was past——they had landed at last,
    With their boxes, portmanteaus, and bags:
Yet at first sight the crew were not pleased with the
    view,
    Which consisted of chasms and crags.

The Bellman perceived that their spirits were low,
    And repeated in musical tone
Some jokes he had kept for a season of woe——
    But the crew would do nothing but groan.

He served out some grog with a liberal hand,
    And bade them sit down on the beach:
And they could not but own that their Captain
        looked grand,
    As he stood and delivered his speech.

"Friends, Romans, and countrymen, lend me
        your ears!"
    (They were all of them fond of quotations:
So they drank to his health, and they gave him
        three cheers,
    While he served out additional rations).

"We have sailed many months, we have sailed
        many weeks
    (Four weeks to the month you may mark),
But never as yet ('tis your Captain who speaks)
    Have we caught the least glimpse of a Snark!

"We have sailed many weeks, we have sailed
        many days
    (Seven days to the week I allow),

But a Snark, on the which we might lovingly gaze,
    We have never beheld till now!

"Come, listen, my men, while I tell you again
    The five unmistakable marks
By which you may know, wheresoever you go,
    The warranted genuine Snarks.

"Let us take them in order.   The first is the taste,
    Which is meagre and hollow, but crisp:
Like a coat that is rather too tight in the waist,
    With a flavour of Will-o'-the-wisp.

"Its habit of getting up late you'll agree
    That it carries too far, when I say
That it frequently breakfasts at five-o'clock tea,
    And dines on the following day.

"The third is its slowness in taking a jest,
    Should you happen to venture on one,
It will sigh like a thing that is deeply distressed:
    And it always looks grave at a pun.

"The fourth is its fondness for bathing-machines,
    Which it constantly carries about,
And believes that they add to the beauty of scenes——
    A sentiment open to doubt.

"The fifth is ambition.   It next will be right
    To describe each particular batch:
Distinguishing those that have feathers, and bite,
    From those that have whiskers, and scratch.

"For, although common Snarks do no manner of harm,
    Yet, I feel it my duty to say,
Some are Boojums——"   The Bellman broke off in
        alarm,
    For the Baker had fainted away.

FIT THE THIRD
The Baker's Tale

They roused him with muffins—they roused him
    with ice—
    They roused him with mustard and cress—
They roused him with jam and judicious advice—
    They set him conundrums to guess.

When at length he sat up and was able to speak,
    His sad story he offered to tell;
And the Bellman cried "Silence! not even a
    shriek!"
    And excitedly tingled his bell.

There was silence supreme!   Not a shriek, not a
    scream,
    Scarcely even a howl or a groan,

As the man they called "Ho!" told his story of woe
   In an antediluvian tone.

"My father and mother were honest, though poor—"
   "Skip all that!" cried the Bellman in haste.

17

"If it once becomes dark, there's no chance of a
  Snark——
  We have hardly a minute to waste!"

"I skip forty years," said the Baker, in tears,
  "And proceed without further remark
To the day when you took me aboard of your ship
  To help you in hunting the Snark.

"A dear uncle of mine (after whom I was named)
  Remarked, when I bade him farewell——"
"Oh, skip your dear uncle!" the Bellman exclaimed,
  As he angrily tingled his bell.

"He remarked to me then," said that mildest of men,
  " 'If your Snark be a Snark, that is right:
Fetch it home by all means——you may serve it
    with greens,
  And it's handy for striking a light.
" 'You may seek it with thimbles——and seek it
    with care;
  You may hunt it with forks and hope;

You may threaten its life with a railway-share;
    You may charm it with smiles and soap—' "

("That's exactly the method," the Bellman bold
    In a hasty parenthesis cried,
"That's exactly the way I have always
        been told
    That the capture of Snarks should be tried!")

" 'But oh, beamish nephew, beware of the day,
    If your Snark be a Boojum!   For then
You will softly and suddenly vanish away,
    And never be met with again!'

"It is this, it is this that oppresses my soul,
    When I think of my uncle's last words:
And my heart is like nothing so much as a bowl
    Brimming over with quivering curds!

"It is this, it is this——"   "We have had that
        before!"
    The Bellman indignantly said.

And the Baker replied "Let me say it once more.
  It is this, it is this that I dread!

"I engage with the Snark——every night after
    dark——
  In a dreamy delirious fight:
I serve it with greens in those shadowy scenes,
  And I use it for striking a light;

"But if ever I meet with a Boojum, that day,
    In a moment (of this I am sure),
I shall softly and suddenly vanish away—
  And the notion I cannot endure!"

FIT THE FOURTH
The Hunting

The Bellman looked uffish, and wrinkled his brow.
   "If only you'd spoken before!
It's excessively awkward to mention it now,
   With the Snark, so to speak, at the door!

"We should all of us grieve, as you well may believe,
   If you never were met with again——
But surely, my man, when the voyage began,
   You might have suggested it then?

"It's excessively awkward to mention it now—
   As I think I've already remarked."
And the man they called "Hi!" replied, with a sigh,
   "I informed you the day we embarked.

"You may charge me with murder—or want of sense—
    (We are all of us weak at times):
But the slightest approach to a false pretence
    Was never among my crimes!

"I said it in Hebrew—I said it in Dutch—
    I said it in German and Greek;

But I wholly forgot (and it vexes me much)
  That English is what you speak!"

"'Tis a pitiful tale," said the Bellman, whose face
  Had grown longer at every word;
"But, now that you've stated the whole of your case,
  More debate would be simply absurd.

"The rest of my speech" (he explained to his men)
  "You shall hear when I've leisure to speak it.
But the Snark is at hand, let me tell you again!
  'Tis your glorious duty to seek it!

"To seek it with thimbles, to seek it with care;
  To pursue it with forks and hope;
To threaten its life with a railway-share;
  To charm it with smiles and soap!

"For the Snark's a peculiar creature, that won't
  Be caught in a commonplace way.
Do all that you know, and try all that you don't:
  Not a chance must be wasted to-day!

"For England expects——I forbear to proceed:
   'Tis a maxim tremendous, but trite:
And you'd best be unpacking the things that you
      need
    To rig yourselves out for the fight."

Then the Banker endorsed a blank cheque
     (which he crossed),
   And changed his loose silver for notes.
The Baker with care combed his whiskers and hair,
   And shook the dust out of his coats.

The Boots and the Broker were sharpening a
     spade—
   Each working the grindstone in turn;
But the Beaver went on making lace, and
     displayed
   No interest in the concern:

Though the Barrister tried to appeal to its pride,
   And vainly proceeded to cite
A number of cases, in which making laces
   Had been proved an infringement of right.

The maker of Bonnets ferociously planned
   A novel arrangement of bows:
While the Billiard-marker with quivering hand
   Was chalking the tip of his nose.

But the Butcher turned nervous, and dressed himself fine,
    With yellow kid gloves and a ruff——
Said he felt it exactly like going to dine,
    Which the Bellman declared was all "stuff."

"Introduce me, now there's a good fellow," he said,
    "If we happen to meet it together!"
And the Bellman, sagaciously nodding his head,
    Said "That must depend on the weather."

The Beaver went simply galumphing about,
    At seeing the Butcher so shy:
And even the Baker, though stupid and stout,
    Made an effort to wink with one eye.

"Be a man!" said the Bellman in wrath, as he heard
    The Butcher beginning to sob.
"Should we meet with a Jubjub, that desperate bird,
    We shall need all our strength for the job!"

FIT THE FIFTH
The Beaver's Lesson

They sought it with thimbles, they sought it with
    care;
    They pursued it with forks and hope;
They threatened its life with a railway-share;
    They charmed it with smiles and soap.

Then the Butcher contrived an ingenious plan
    For making a separate sally;
And had fixed on a spot unfrequented by man,
    A dismal and desolate valley.

But the very same plan to the Beaver occurred:
    It had chosen the very same place;
Yet neither betrayed, by a sign or a word,
    The disgust that appeared in his face.

Each thought he was thinking of nothing but
       "Snark"
   And the glorious work of the day;
And each tried to pretend that he did not remark
   That the other was going that way.

But the valley grew narrow and narrower still,
   And the evening got darker and colder,
Till (merely from nervousness, not from
       goodwill)
   They marched along shoulder to shoulder.

Then a scream, shrill and high, rent the
       shuddering sky,
   And they knew that some danger was near:
The Beaver turned pale to the tip of its tail,
   And even the Butcher felt queer.

He thought of his childhood, left far far behind—
   That blissful and innocent state—
The sound so exactly recalled to his mind
   A pencil that squeaks on a slate!

"'Tis the voice of the Jubjub!" he suddenly cried.
  (This man, that they used to call "Dunce.")
"As the Bellman would tell you," he added with
      pride,
    "I have uttered that sentiment once.

"'Tis the note of the Jubjub! Keep count, I entreat;
  You will find I have told it you twice.
'Tis the song of the Jubjub!   The proof is
      complete,
    If only I've stated it thrice."

The Beaver had counted with scrupulous care,
  Attending to every word:
But it fairly lost heart, and outgrabe in despair,
  When the third repetition occurred.

It felt that, in spite of all possible pains,
  It had somehow contrived to lose count,
And the only thing now was to rack its poor
      brains
    By reckoning up the amount.

"Two added to one—if that could but be done,"
    It said, "with one's fingers and thumbs!"
Recollecting with tears how, in earlier years,
    It had taken no pains with its sums.

"The thing can be done," said the Butcher, "I
        think.
    The thing must be done, I am sure.
The thing shall be done! Bring me paper and ink,
    The best there is time to procure."

The Beaver brought paper, portfolio, pens,
    And ink in unfailing supplies:
While strange creepy creatures came out of their
        dens,
    And watched them with wondering eyes.

So engrossed was the Butcher, he heeded them not,
    As he wrote with a pen in each hand,
And explained all the while in a popular style
    Which the Beaver could well understand.

"Taking Three as the subject to reason about——
    A convenient number to state——
We add Seven, and Ten, and then multiply out
    By One Thousand diminished by Eight.

"The result we proceed to divide, as you see,
    By Nine Hundred and Ninety and Two:
Then subtract Seventeen, and the answer
        must be
    Exactly and perfectly true.

"The method employed I would gladly explain,
    While I have it so clear in my head,
If I had but the time and you had but the brain——
    But much yet remains to be said.

"In one moment I've seen what has hitherto been
    Enveloped in absolute mystery,
And without extra charge I will give you
        at large
    A Lesson in Natural History."

In his genial way he proceeded to say
   (Forgetting all laws of propriety,
And that giving instruction, without introduction,
   Would have caused quite a thrill in Society),

"As to temper the Jubjub's a desperate bird,
   Since it lives in perpetual passion:
Its taste in costume is entirely absurd——
   It is ages ahead of the fashion:

"But it knows any friend it has met once before:
   It never will look at a bribe:
And in charity-meetings it stands at the door,
   And collects——though it does not subscribe.

"Its flavour when cooked is more exquisite far
   Than mutton, or oysters, or eggs:
(Some think it keeps best in an ivory jar,
   And some, in mahogany kegs:

"You boil it in sawdust: you salt it in glue:
   You condense it with locusts and tape:

Still keeping one principal object in view——
    To preserve its symmetrical shape."

The Butcher would gladly have talked till next
        day,
    But he felt that the Lesson must end,
And he wept with delight in attempting to say
    He considered the Beaver his friend.

While the Beaver confessed, with affectionate
        looks
    More eloquent even than tears,
It had learnt in ten minutes far more than all
        books
    Would have taught it in seventy years.

They returned hand-in-hand, and the Bellman,
        unmanned
    (For a moment) with noble emotion,
Said "This amply repays all the wearisome
        days
    We have spent on the billowy ocean!"

Such friends, as the Beaver and Butcher became,
    Have seldom if ever been known;
In winter or summer, 'twas always the same——
    You could never meet either alone.

And when quarrels arose——as one frequently finds
    Quarrels will, spite of every endeavour——
The song of the Jubjub recurred to their minds,
    And cemented their friendship for ever!

FIT THE SIXTH

The Barrister's Dream

They sought it with thimbles, they sought it with
  care;
  They pursued it with forks and hope;
They threatened its life with a railway-share;
  They charmed it with smiles and soap.

But the Barrister, weary of proving in vain
  That the Beaver's lace-making was wrong,
Fell asleep, and in dreams saw the creature quite
  plain
  That his fancy had dwelt on so long.

He dreamed that he stood in a shadowy Court,
  Where the Snark, with a glass in its eye,
Dressed in gown, bands, and wig, was defending
  a pig
  On the charge of deserting its sty.

The Witnesses proved, without error or flaw,
    That the sty was deserted when found:
And the Judge kept explaining the state of the law
    In a soft under-current of sound.

The indictment had never been clearly expressed,
    And it seemed that the Snark had begun,
And had spoken three hours, before any one guessed
    What the pig was supposed to have done.

The Jury had each formed a different view
   (Long before the indictment was read),
And they all spoke at once, so that none of them
      knew
      One word that the others had said.

"You must know——" said the Judge: but the
      Snark exclaimed "Fudge!
   That statute is obsolete quite!
Let me tell you, my friends, the whole question
      depends
      On an ancient manorial right.

"In the matter of Treason the pig would appear
   To have aided, but scarcely abetted:
While the charge of Insolvency fails, it is clear,
   If you grant the plea 'never indebted.'

"The fact of Desertion I will not dispute:
   But its guilt, as I trust, is removed
(So far as relates to the costs of this suit)
   By the Alibi which has been proved.

"My poor client's fate now depends on your votes."
  Here the speaker sat down in his place,
And directed the Judge to refer to his notes
  And briefly to sum up the case.

But the Judge said he never had summed up before;
  So the Snark undertook it instead,
And summed it so well that it came to far more
  Than the Witnesses ever had said!

When the verdict was called for, the Jury declined,
  As the word was so puzzling to spell;
But they ventured to hope that the Snark wouldn't
    mind
  Undertaking that duty as well.

So the Snark found the verdict, although, as it
    owned,
  It was spent with the toils of the day:
When it said the word "GUILTY!" the Jury all
    groaned,
  And some of them fainted away.

Then the Snark pronounced sentence, the Judge
    being quite
    Too nervous to utter a word:
When it rose to its feet, there was silence like night,
    And the fall of a pin might be heard.

"Transportation for life" was the sentence it
    gave,
    "And *then* to be fined forty pound."
The Jury all cheered, though the Judge said he
    feared
    That the phrase was not legally sound.

But their wild exultation was suddenly checked
    When the jailer informed them, with tears,
Such a sentence would have not the slightest effect,
    As the pig had been dead for some years.

The Judge left the Court, looking deeply disgusted:
    But the Snark, though a little aghast,
As the lawyer to whom the defence was intrusted,
    Went bellowing on to the last.

Thus the Barrister dreamed, while the bellowing
    seemed
  To grow every moment more clear:
Till he woke to the knell of a furious bell,
  Which the Bellman rang close at his ear.

FIT THE SEVENTH
The Banker's Fate

They sought it with thimbles, they sought it with
    care;
    They pursued it with forks and hope;
They threatened its life with a railway-share;
    They charmed it with smiles and soap.

And the Banker, inspired with a courage so new
    It was matter for general remark,
Rushed madly ahead and was lost to their view
    In his zeal to discover the Snark.

But while he was seeking with thimbles and care,
    A Bandersnatch swiftly drew nigh
And grabbed at the Banker, who shrieked in despair,
    For he knew it was useless to fly.

He offered large discount—he offered a cheque
    (Drawn "to bearer") for seven-pounds-ten:
But the Bandersnatch merely extended its neck
    And grabbed at the Banker again.

Without rest or pause—while those frumious jaws
    Went savagely snapping around—
He skipped and he hopped, and he floundered
        and flopped,
    Till fainting he fell to the ground.

The Bandersnatch fled as the others appeared:
    Led on by that fear-stricken yell:
And the Bellman remarked "It is just as I feared!"
    And solemnly tolled on his bell.

He was black in the face, and they scarcely could
        trace
    The least likeness to what he had been:
While so great was his fright that his waistcoat
        turned white—
    A wonderful thing to be seen!

To the horror of all who were present that day,
  He uprose in full evening dress,
And with senseless grimaces endeavoured to say
  What his tongue could no longer express.

Down he sank in a chair—ran his hands through
    his hair—
  And chanted in mimsiest tones
Words whose utter inanity proved his insanity,
  While he rattled a couple of bones.

"Leave him here to his fate—it is getting so
    late!"
  The Bellman exclaimed in a fright.
"We have lost half the day. Any further delay,
  And we sha'n't catch a Snark before night!"

FIT THE EIGHTH
The Vanishing

They sought it with thimbles, they sought it with
    care;
    They pursued it with forks and hope;
They threatened its life with a railway-share;
    They charmed it with smiles and soap.

They shuddered to think that the chase might fail,
    And the Beaver, excited at last,
Went bounding along on the tip of its tail,
    For the daylight was nearly past.

"There is Thingumbob shouting!" the Bellman said.
    "He is shouting like mad, only hark!
He is waving his hands, he is wagging his head,
    He has certainly found a Snark!"

They gazed in delight, while the Butcher
    exclaimed
    "He was always a desperate wag!"
They beheld him—their Baker—their hero
    unnamed—
    On the top of a neighbouring crag,

Erect and sublime, for one moment of time.
    In the next, that wild figure they saw
(As if stung by a spasm) plunge into a chasm,
    While they waited and listened in awe.

"It's a Snark!" was the sound that first came to
    their ears,
    And seemed almost too good to be true.
Then followed a torrent of laughter and cheers:
    Then the ominous words "It's a Boo—"

Then, silence. Some fancied they heard in the air
    A weary and wandering sigh
That sounded like "—jum!" but the others declare
    It was only a breeze that went by.

They hunted till darkness came on, but they
    found
  Not a button, or feather, or mark,
By which they could tell that they stood on the
    ground
  Where the Baker had met with the Snark.

In the midst of the word he was trying to say
  In the midst of his laughter and glee,
He had softly and suddenly vanished away——
  For the Snark *was* a Boojum, you see.

THE END